To,

The Eye Clinic

With Best wishes

Anwar
16/12/24

CW01648061

WORD BIRDS

WORD BIRDS

KHALID ANWER

Other books by Khalid Anwer

Music of Ideas

Thoughtful Reflections

A Little Bit of Randomness

I ate the Sun Rays with a Fork Today

Fractured through Time

Humanity Perplexity

101 Love Poems

Like A Cuckoo Clock

I Like the World I Look At

Photon

Time spent with words, should be like time spent with friends, with joy, conviviality and without urgency. The memory generated lingers on forever.

It is such a delight for a writer that when you spend so much time in the company of words, you become fascinated, captivated, endeared, enamoured, enriched, fulfilled and blessed by them.

I let my words be

They have

A laissez faire upbringing

Weightless Words Work Wonders

Table of Contents

Word Birds

Morning time is the most delightful time for
the birds
they are most happy, busy and chirpy at the
heralding light
flying from tree to tree.
On my morning walk I noticed that they
chirped to their heart's delight
while sitting on the tree. As soon they take
to the air, the chirping stops
as if by an unspoken rule.
Is it to avoid confusion, collision
or just to keep the flying experience honest.
The word birds behave differently
they sit silently, patiently, eagerly
waiting to be tagged
as soon as you start reading
they take wing, come alive
chirping, singing, sweeping
you are their ventriloquist

the glass blower, the conductor
there is cacophony of noise
there is magic in the air
there is music in the air
guitars are strumming
drums are drumming
and then it all stops
when you stop.

I Know Why the Words Sing

it is a symphony

as the feet dance in company

as the hands clap in unison

as the clouds float together

as the stars twinkle at night

as the water vapours roar

as the rainbows colour the sky

as the planets rotate the sun

as the electrons revolve the nucleus

as the kingfishers dive

as the butterflies float

as the robins do a mud bath

words are joyous in each other's company

the songs are a celebration

a frisson

a delight

a harmony

a thrill

and as the birds sing for love

for territory, for the seasons

for being alive

the words sing for all those reasons and much
more

Heirloom

I keep collecting new words
to add to my vocabulary
to vary my repertoire
as if someday, they will
become a precious heirloom
they also have a different role
when the life's boat is on a roll
provide the buoyancy to the boat
and keep life's boat afloat

Words Have Feelings Too

They are on their best behaviour
Very smart, elegant and ornate
Carrying little flags
Displaying, meaning, associations
Some even their Etymologies
Very eager to be picked up
There are whoops of delight
High fives, little waltz
On the selection.
Then there is the time for revision of the
draft
Not the easiest time for a writer
You get so attached to your writing
It sends a shudder down every words spine
As Hemmingway has succinctly put
“kill your little darlings”
some have to go
they barricade themselves
chain themselves with other words

you have to tread carefully
to avoid catastrophe, mutiny
you have to explain to them
a solemn promise that they would be used
soon
would be given a prominent place
You have to give them your word
And a word is a writer's reputation
Words have feelings too

Melody in the Words

Melody is in the words
Melody is in the thoughts
Visual beauty is in the words
Aesthetic beauty is in the thoughts
Perceptual beauty is in the words
Conceptual beauty is in the poem

Words are Like Popcorn

Words are like popcorn
they pop and crackle
with energy and excitement
and with their sweet- sour
bitter-tangy, piquancy
give you company
and be a candid witness
to the movie of your life
enfold in front of your eyes
on the big screen of life
and can relate to the stories
being told in varied words

Words are like Popcorn

Interlocking Words

Interlocking words
Intermingling words
Criss-crossing words
Intertwining words
Interweaving words
Inexplicable words
Incontrovertible words
Immutable words
Irrevocable words
Irreparable words
Indelible words
Iridescent words

No Word is Without its Reverberations

memory

history

visibility

past

present

future

Anvil

There is a crowd gathered
Around the anvil
They are like the walking wounded
Few reclining, some lying on the grass
Others making themselves into stretchers
Ferrying the distraught ones
Some are incredibly crestfallen
Used and abused they have become
Clichéd, hackneyed
Few are wistful as they were
In vogue once and now
New and young ones have taken over
Some are mournful and dejected
As their difficult spelling
Is a definite put off
Some are angry that they are
Used out of context
And utterly misunderstood
You have to deal with them

Gently, carefully
Some require a bit of talk therapy
Some require minor adjustments
Few require delicate sewing up to
Mend their broken soul
Few are hammer junkies
Not satisfied until
Enjoyed some heavy blows
At the anvil

Freshly Baked

The aroma rekindles emotions
Evokes memories
I can see a child
Holding his father's hand
Inside the bakery
Father busy talking to the baker
Boy's eyes wide with delight
At eye level to the delicious
Cream horns, muffins, pastries and cakes
Synonymous to the delight
Excitement, exhilaration
Of the writer enjoying
The ecstatic aroma
Of the freshly baked
Words

Instructions

Be courteous, polite,
To your teachers, mentors
Respectful to your seniors
Be generous to your friends
Show humility in receiving praise
Show generosity in giving praise
Magnanimity in forgiveness
Show, eagerness, keenness
To learn, explore, to expand
Keep good company
As you are known by the
Company you keep
Help each other with fortitude
Spread happiness,
Where you find sadness
Spread humour
Where you find dryness
Spread hope
Where you find despair
Spread optimism
Where you find dejection
If you have setbacks
Take it on your metaphorical chin
Work to spread, peace, harmony
Tranquillity in the world

Remember the ephemeral
Nature of it all
On the time's page
A brief existence
And remember to keep
The promises made
As Word is your reputation

My instructions to my
Words

Humming Words

Aerobically aesthetic
figure of eight
flying upside down
backwards
standing still
in conjunction with the moment
joy
the ideas of nectar

Poker Faced Words

Words are the best of poker players
they can read human emotions well
this innate ability to decipher
the subtlest of ciphers
the furrowed forehead
the raised eyebrow
the quivering lip
even involuntary pupillary hippus
accurate predictor of inner turmoil
the link between, thought and emotion
the in between state of decision-indecision
words know to hold their secrets
they know when to enfold them
you cannot glean anything staring
at a word's face, it's only when
they link and join the others
their joy is palpable and the expression
could be read in between the lines
Poker faced Words!

Élan is an Elegant Word

Élan is an elegant word
Exquisite is an exciting word
Eclectic is an electric word
Profuse is a profound word
Fragrance is fragrant word
Timorous is a timid word
Fastidious is a studious word
Uxorious is a luxurious word
Elite is an elitist word
Delete is a deleterious word
Serendipity is a fortuitous word
Facetious is a facile word
Fashion is a fashionable word
Passion is a passionate word
Love is a lovely word

There is an Image Behind Every Word

There is an image behind every word
There is an idea behind every word
There is a story behind every word
The association behind every word
There is music behind every word
There is a motif behind every word
There is magic behind every word
There is mystery behind every word
There are words behind every word
There are worlds behind every word
There is ersatz behind every word
There is élan behind every word
There is zeitgeist among the words
There is meaning in between the lines
There is an image behind every word!

A Rainbow of Words

Abstractionists throw paint at the canvas
Let it flow
Then with a blade
Shape it
Harness it
Poets are no different
They take out the words
From the bucket
And chuck them on the canvass
Some squeal
Others thud
Some slide
Some glide
Some flow
Some glow
Some gash
Some dash
Some bash
Some streak

Some freak

Some linger

Some whisper

Some whimper

Some are sad

Some are glad

Some roar

Some cower

Some flower

There is the

Poem

Painted for you

A rainbow of words

A Game of Blindfold

Game Of Blindfold
We love this game
Taking turns
First the words
Blindfold me
And they give me a word
I have to give a detail description
Creating the right atmosphere
Depicting in the picture they are holding
Then it is my turn
I put the blindfold quite tight
So there is no chance of peeking
And then I describe a scene
And they have to proffer a single
Word , depicting, capturing the
Whole scene

Ah! The games we play!

Where Do Words Come From

Where do words come from
where the ideas go
and send images as if
post cards being sent
from exotic places
unbelievable journeys
magical action
and these images are
transcribed into little
squiggles of ink
to recapture the essence of it all
word is an image itself
a whole world immersed in it

The Cure

An injection of few verses
A dose of few metaphors
A sip of similes
A spoonful of assonance
An aliquot of alliteration
A mouthful of Motif
An instant of images
An infinity of ideas
Words are antidote
Stopping the spread of epidemic
Only cure is literary and academic!

Words do not like to be Blindfolded

Words Do Not Like To Be Blindfolded
They want to see the world with their own
eyes
To visit places
To go on a journey
To go for an adventure
To play with their own kind
To form associations
To form friendships
To fall in love
Have their own altercations
Have ways to find peace, tranquillity,
harmony
To write their own lyrics
To sing their own songs
Once blindfolded they get stunned
They know that the quicker they reveal the
secret
Where have they been,

what have they been up to

The quicker I will remove the blindfold

Words Do Not Like To Be Blindfolded

Ballad of the Sad Café

Ballad of the sad café
Is not the same as
Salad of the bad café
Celibate
Is not the same as
Celebrate
Beware of the letter
You omit

I am Ready

I am ready for the provocation
Thoughts provoke you
Images provoke you
Ideas provoke you
Sights provoke you
Visions provoke you
Dreams provoke you
Motif provokes you
Motives provoke you
Music provokes you
Sound provokes you
Rhythm provokes you
Silence provokes you
Smiles provoke you
Glances provoke you
Flowers provoke you
Comments provoke you
Beauty provokes you
Beguile provokes you

Truth provokes you
Innocence provokes you
Kindness provokes you
Altruism provokes you
Mystery provokes you
Cosmos provokes you
Love Evokes you
I am ready for the provocation
I am ready with my WORDS

As Old As

As old as books
As deep as rivers
As old as stars
As deep as space
As comfortable as a glove
As delicate as love
As delightful as a new word

Ah! What are Similes Like

Ah! What are Similes Like
What are metaphor for
What does Alliteration repeat
What does Ellipsis... Omit
What does Oxymoron contradict
What does
Allusion allude
Allegory personify
Assonance sound
Analogy illustrate
Metonymy replaces
Parable teach
Mnemonic remembers
Onomatopoeia imitate
Muse inspire
Paradigm shift
Parody mocks
Satire ridicules
Myth propagates
Plagiarism steals
Renaissance rebirths
Synaesthesia combines
Synonym substitutes
Stanza separates
Ballad sings

Elegy laments
Dialogue speaks
Emblem pictures
Enjambment runs over
Epigram wits
Eponymous names
Fable morals
Grotesque bizarre
Caesuras pause
Ah! What are Similes like
Ah! What the poet poems!

Word Affair

Writing is a hot affair
periods of exhilaration
anxiety, apprehension
delirium, hope, joy, fear, despair
each word is chosen with
diligence to have the maximum
impact, it is a gamble, and as every
gambler knows, how to keep the
cards close, play poker faced
reading the face for the clues
for the subtle signs in the eyes
knows when to put the arms around
to complement, to praise,
to ignore the tantrums
and may be throw one or two of yours
but in this game the words are always the
winner
as they have the secret ace up their sleeves
King of the words
Love
Word Affair!

Sometimes the Dust is the Best Thing Words Can Eat

Sometimes the dust is the best thing the
words can eat
Sometimes darkness is the only place the
words feel cool
Sometimes left alone words could gather
their thoughts
Sometimes left alone words could find their
own space
Sometimes left alone words could find their
own voice
Sometimes left alone words could find their
own tune
Sometimes left alone words could find their
own songs
Sometimes left alone words could dance
their own dance
Sometimes left alone words could start
telling themselves a story

Sometimes it is best to write something and
leave it for
Six months and then revisit it
You are a different person
And so are the words, you may
Find that the ending may be the new
beginning
Sometimes dust is the best thing the words
can eat

Wonder

I wonder
why
in the
company
of my
Photons
I feel
so
illuminated
and in the company
of my new words
I am so excited

Image

Let us make it plain
Like the heart beats
The heart contains
And the emotions
It tries to reign
And the mind
Self control trains
It is not the what
The heart beats learn
It is the Image
The heart retains
It is the word that refrains

Map

Map the wind

Map the sky

Map the stars

Map the water

Map the emotions

Map the beauty

Map the truth

Map the elegance

Map the mind

Map the soul

Map the heart

Map the love

Map the word

Lingua Franca

Language of darkness
Language of prejudice
Language of silence
Language of emotions
Language of wisdom
Language of dreams
Language of truth
Language of the Universe
Language of the atom
Language of Love
Language of Words

Vagaries

Elegance of beauty

Elegance of truth

Elegance of joy

Elegance of laughter

Elegance of friendship

Elegance of words

Borderline Personality of Words

Narcissistic

Flamboyant

Introvert

Extrovert

Whimsical

Maladroit

Malaprop

Audacious

Ostentatious

Uxorious

What to tell the Words

How to read the Air
How to read the water
How to read the mind
How to read the fire
How to read the sky
How to read the universe
What to tell the heart
What to tell the words

Every Word Has a Sound

every word has a sound

even silence

and echoes abound

mostly silent

but how profound

Words Have History

Words have mystery
What I call Father
Is also called Pater
What I call Water
Is also called Wasser
And Daughter is Dughater

Playing With Words

Who says relinquish instead of give up
who says confounding instead of confusing

who says I am admiring instead of liking
who says do you realise instead of you know

who says I'd rather instead I would like to
who says shield my eyes instead of cover
my eyes

who is playing with words and having fun
this must be Anum

Sparklers

Words like sparklers
sparkle like words
in the darkness of humanity
glimmer like bulbs
delightful ambience
a surreal glow
just like life in all directions flow
although only arms length away
just like life no control to sway
you think magic would forever last
but the photons soon lose their blast
and you are standing in the abysmal dark
hearing your heart beats
waiting for the next delicious, exquisite
spark

Eye Tooth

Words settle on my brain
And the brain settles on the words
As a hen settles on eggs
EYETOOTH
High truth of
Hen with a tooth

Bouquet

I love colours
My retina love colours
I love flowers
As flowers are full of colours
I love bouquets
An emotional croquet
I love to receive bouquets
even more delighted to send them
To loved one and friends
As I know the perfect reason
To send a bouquet
Is no reason at all
How I wish to send
More of them more often
Then an epiphany
I can use my words
As the most fragrant of flowers
Arrange them in a bouquet of a poem
And with the click of a button
Can send it to anyone and everyone
Anywhere in the world
They would always remain fresh
The only watering and pruning
Is through the eyes

And each time they would appear
More fresh more profound
As if when you were not looking
The flowers have re arranged themselves
Into a different pattern
A more delightful design
As if trying to reveal
A different more subtle
Message on further reading
This is my bouquet for you
I know it would remain fresh
Or at least the fragrance
Would linger on
While the music plays on

We Encounter Each Other in Words

We encounter each other in words
We decipher each other in silences
We know each other in smiles
We hear each other in touch
We feel each other in eyes
We fall for each other in love

Mind Starts Working

Mind starts working
Whetted by thought
Eyes start shining
Whetted by sight
Lips start quivering
Whetted by words
Heart stars beating
Whetted by love

Reticence

Reticence
Silences
Restraints
Hesitations
In the commas
In the dashes
In the space between the words
And the sibilants ant at the ends
And words seem to hang there
Not to end
Or not to end too easily

Words Neatly Aligned

Poetry is jingling pieces of string
Waiting for someone to strum and string
Words neatly aligned
A deep creative well do spring
And when it starts to play
Your heart is tickled by a soft string
And then it vibrates with your frequency
Your heart begins to sing
And you wonder
It indeed is
Amazing!

Love of Words

To have a great love
respect
enthusiasm
fondness
wonder
awe
splendour
intrigue
and friendliness for words.
To enjoy their antics
their misdemeanour
their magic
their mischief
their courage
valour and chivalry.
Their sense of adventure
the quest for pilgrimage
their search for meaning
knowledge
wisdom
truth.
The sense of conviction
coming together
in need of sorrow
grief
sadness
to console
comfort
encourage

enthuse
effuse
support
or just lend a hearing ear
a crying shoulder.
They have a natural gift to say words
that would lift your spirit up
your heart soar
to make you oblivious of all the trivialities
to make you understand the deep meaning of life
to look at the bigger picture
to contemplate
to ponder
to wonder
to search for the meaning of it all
where we have come from
where we are going.
Then words find
most surreal of place in a mother's heart
expression of tenderness
exquisite care
inextricably linked
to most endurable of relations
that indelible mark
that a child leaves on her heart
a place of solace
of profound joy
of serene tranquillity.
As insatiable love as it can be.
The words in a father's mouth

may appear stern
abrasive
it is to impart a sense of toughness
a duty of care
to teach tough lessons of life
to impart experience
wisdom
through stories
fable
allegory.
It can be a tough love
but most enigmatic love it sure is.
Thinking of friends
a relationship so unique
so otherworldly
so pure
so fragrant
so delightful
so capacious
And then thinking about love
a sweet frisson envelopes
a trance
an elegance
a charm
beauty
a paradox
most tantalising
from the most quotidian
to the most grandeur
an intertwine like no other
most mysterious of entanglements

most marvellous of sentiments
delirious!
Then come to think of the brain
the vagaries of the human mind
the allure
the indescribable thought process
the indiscernible pursuit of truth
the unfathomable vastness
the mysterious pique of interest
a piquant sense of humour.
The teachers that use the words are so
precious
so important, to form the personality
to firm the character
a transition from doubt to confidence
from timorous to pillar of strength.
If one realises the power of the words
how deeply they influence you
both consciously and subconsciously or
conscientiously
one would only use positive words
let the heart be joyous
let the mind be clear
let the spirit soar
let the words delight

Until Calm Prevails

As bees are calmed by smoke
As bears are calmed by a scratching
As babies are calmed by lullaby
As children are calmed by play
As partners are calmed by praise
As lions are calmed by non-eye contact
As acid is calmed by alkali
As fire is calmed by water
As alligators are calmed by blindfold
As snake is calmed by charming
The heart is calmed by words
And mind by an intellectual poem
Until Calm Prevails

To

To travel
to marvel
to explore
to deplore
to etch
to sketch
to paint
to draw
to inspire
to perspire
to entertain
to walk
to talk
to laugh
to giggle
to cry
to worry
to eat
to drink
to work
to befriend
to help
to remember
to forgive
to forgo
to admit
to express
to promise
to Carry

to arrive
to anticipate
to sleep
to wake
to stars
to heaven
to galaxies
to butterflies
to Romance
to love
to anticipate
Words keep you company
On this electable journey

Strange Juxtapositions

Menage
Melange
Eschewed
Chewed
Keen
Eager
Meant
Embodiment
Rapturous
Rupture
Immature
Imprimatur
Wheedle
Waddle
Weave
Wave
Nebulous
Bullous
Camera
Obscura

Weighing Scale for Words

Writers have an exquisite scale for words
as an expert chef knows that the weight of
ingredients
their texture, their colour is very important
and crucial
one light word can be quite heavy
and heavy words can be quite light
some simple words can be abrasive
some simple words can be deceptive
some words can be so resplendent, fragrant
some are delightfully diaphanous
some are delicate, others can be rococo,
baroque, ornate
some can be gelatinous, mutinous
some capacious, some capricious
some perineal, some pernicious
some alliterative, some sibilant
some sonorous, some monotonous
some allegoric, some metaphoric

some incredible, some indelible
some splendid, some candid
some semantic, some oxymoronic
some cooperative, some hesitant
some jubilant, some vigilant
some inquire, some perspire
some piquant, some picaroon,
some peek, some pique
some audacious, some ostentatious
some adventurous, some maverick.
And as boxers are weighed before the fight
to confirm their category
or as a chemist diligently weighs the
ingredients
for the perfect inviolable mix
or a jeweller weighs for precision
each word is scrutinised for its height,
its size, sound, colour, texture, its weight
and then they are put together
for the delightful recipe
Compliments to the CHEF!

Ballet

It begins with small tentative steps
literally finding your feet
cautious of tripping, wrong footing
less sure of the movement
of the message being conveyed.
Then as the confidence grows
movement flows
becoming smooth, effortless, graceful
a friend commented on my writing
'Look how it has changed
it began small and now it has
become fat and chunky
it seems you were in full flow.'
Indeed, it also starts with
small tentative sentences
short phrases
unsure of the message
but as the confidence grows

movement becomes effortless, graceful

the writing becomes bulky, fattens

you lose yourself

It is Ballet on the page

No pretence

Just the flow!

A Poet is Like a Jeweller

A poet is like a jeweller
The words are his Jewels
The diamonds, precious metals
He knows how to use
Them with precision
Laser precision
To contrast them
To match them
Big heavy ones
Go with little
Delicate ones
More radiant ones go
With less resplendent ones
And sometimes one single
Big one is enough on its own
And then they are lined up
To form a very delicate
Ornate necklace
As if each word is hanging for its life
With their finger tips

Wild Horses

New words are like wild horses
grazing at the periphery
always alert, afraid
ready to bolt
as anxious of you
as you are daunted by them
no amount of lasso would
control them, catch them
if you try to catch them forcibly
they will kick you
where it hurts most
pride goes before the fall
it is best to let them
mingle with your tamed ones
they get familiar,
they get accustomed
then even if you are not trying
not looking
they would nudge you

beckon you

to ride them

bare feet

bareback

and lead you full trot

to the horizon

to elation!

For comments, critique and suggestions:

skanwer@gmail.com

About the Author

Khalid has been living in Newcastle-under-Lyme, for the past thirty years.
He was born in Karachi.
A practicing Ophthalmologist.
Has a great love for Literature, art and drama.
Fascinated by physics, particularly quantum mechanics.
Intrigued by cosmos, by bird migration, the mystery of sleep,
the marvels of the human brain.
The poems are an amalgam of his deep interests, the musings of an inquiring mind, to make the sense of it all.
Our beginnings, the origin of time and space, the intricacies of the particles
an electable façade, hiding the true reality.
Khalid writes about human interactions, the delights of the written and spoken word.
And indeed about the most ubiquitous of things, love.
Transcendental Love.

Printed in Great Britain
by Amazon

53652758R00090